IT HAPPENED TO ME

Having an

# EATING DISORDER

WITHDRAWN

## Stories from Survivors

SARAH EASON AND SARAH LEVETE

CHERITON
CHILDREN'S BOOKS

Please visit our website, www.cheritonchildrensbooks.com to see more of our high-quality books.

First Edition

Published in 2022 by Cheriton Children's Books
PO Box 7258, Bridgnorth, Shropshire, WV16 9ET, UK

© 2022 Cheriton Children's Books

Authors: Sarah Eason and Sarah Levete
Designer: Paul Myerscough
Editor: Jennifer Sanderson
Picture Researcher: Rachel Blount
Proofreader: Tracey Kelly

Printed in the United States of America

Publisher's Note: The stories in this book are fictional stories based on extensive research of real-life experiences.

# CONTENTS

# CHAPTER ONE

# WHEN EATING IS A STRUGGLE

Everyone needs to eat food. Food provides the body with fuel and **nourishment**. When people are hungry, they eat to give their bodies energy. The **nutrients** in that food also provide the substances that the body needs to perform all the many tasks it does each day, from repairing tissues to carrying blood to different organs in the body. Eating also gives people pleasure —when food is delicious, it makes people feel good and satisfied, and it is sociable to enjoy food with family and friends. However, for some people, eating is a problem rather than a pleasure or necessity. For them, food has become a **mechanism** to cope with painful emotions, and eating is a struggle.

## WHAT IS AN EATING DISORDER?

When a person has issues and difficulties surrounding food, they are **diagnosed** with having an eating disorder. Someone with an eating disorder is **obsessed** with what they can and cannot eat. They are very concerned about their weight and their own and others' body images. It is possible for anyone to develop an eating disorder, however, no one can catch one. They are not infectious diseases. Instead, an eating disorder often starts as a diet, but it gets out of control. It then develops into an unhealthy attitude to food.

The teenage years can be tough. Both boys and girls may develop eating disorders during this challenging time.

## WHAT IS IT LIKE TO HAVE AN EATING DISORDER?

Many people who suffer from an eating disorder feel that no one understands them and what they are going through. They often feel isolated from the rest of the world and all alone with their problem. Having an eating disorder is very lonely, confusing, and painful.

*Having an eating disorder can be difficult to talk about. This can make sufferers feel even more alone with their problems.*

# It Happened to Me

This book follows the "It Happened to Me" fictional journals of different young people who have an eating disorder. These stories from survivors explain what it is like to struggle with food, and how having an eating disorder happened to them. The conclusions to their stories on pages 44-45 also show that it is possible to overcome an eating disorder and lead a happy and fulfilling life. The stories and information in this book can support people suffering from eating disorders and help everyone better understand them.

## BEING ANOREXIC

Some people suffer from an eating disorder known as anorexia nervosa, which is usually called just anorexia. They drastically restrict, or cut back, their food intake in order to lose weight and to weigh as little as possible. When those suffering from anorexia look at themselves in the mirror, they do not see an accurate reflection—they think they look overweight, even if they are shockingly underweight. Anorexia is a serious mental illness that can cause great harm to the health of people who suffer from the condition. In severe cases, anorexia can be fatal, or lead to loss of life.

*Anorexia is not about being on a diet to look slim. Instead, sufferers are dangerously underweight.*

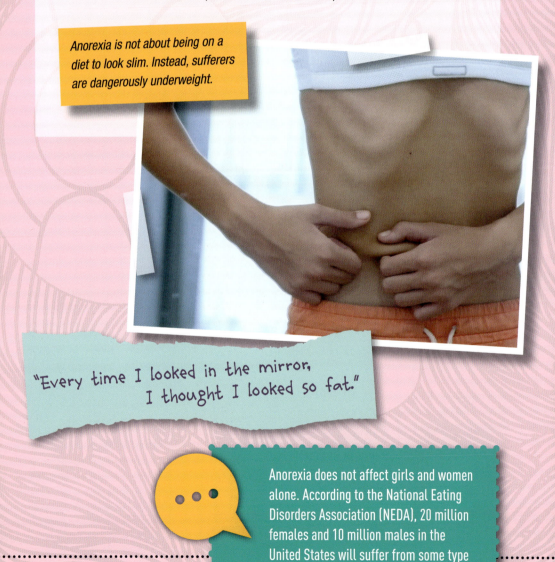

"Every time I looked in the mirror, I thought I looked so fat."

Anorexia does not affect girls and women alone. According to the National Eating Disorders Association (NEDA), 20 million females and 10 million males in the United States will suffer from some type of eating disorder during their lives.

## FRIGHTENED OF FAT

One day of a person cutting back on meals and watching their **calorie** intake in order to lose weight is not anorexia. Instead, anorexia often develops from a diet that gets out of control. Denying the body essential food over a few weeks can develop into anorexia. When this happens, the diet is no longer about losing a few pounds, but, instead it has become an intense fear of becoming fat. The illness takes hold, and the sufferer becomes obsessed with restricting their diet and losing even more weight.

People who suffer from anorexia are terrified of food. They often figure out the calories in every mouthful they eat. Sufferers sometimes chew their food but then spit it out, unable to bear the thought of extra calories that they think will make them fat. They may even reject a sip of water, believing that even this will add to their weight. Often, people with anorexia pretend to eat or say that they have already eaten to avoid consuming food in public. Sufferers wear baggy clothes to hide their skeletal frame so that no one can see how thin they have become.

## IT HAPPENED TO THEM

Those in the modeling industry are often required to be a certain weight, so that designers' clothes fit them perfectly and look as good as possible. However, this means that many models suffer from eating disorders. Former Victoria's Secret model Bridget Malcom has revealed how years of restricting her food and overexercising harmed her health. The 26-year-old model says that at the height of her modeling career, she was constantly exhausted due to lack of food and suffered from anxiety. Bridget says that, even today, she is still dealing with the effects of her eating disorder and that her digestive system is damaged as a result. The model urges everyone to eat healthily and nourish their bodies rather than starve them.

## BEING BULIMIC

Some people suffer from the eating disorder bulimia nervosa. It is usually known as bulimia. Sufferers often appear to be a regular weight, and to outsiders, these sufferers seem healthy. As a result, their eating disorders may continue in secret for a long time before family or friends become aware of them. Like those suffering from anorexia nervosa, bulimics have an agonizing relationship with food. However, bulimics do not starve themselves; instead, they **binge** on large amounts of food and then get rid of it by making themselves vomit or taking **laxatives** to go to the bathroom. This process of ridding the body of food is called purging.

A person who suffers from bulimia may seem to eat normally with family and friends. However, they then secretly purge their body.

Anorexia nervosa and bulimia nervosa, respectively, affect 0.5 percent and 2 to 3 percent of women over their lifetime. The most common age these eating disorders begin is between the ages of 12 and 25. Although much more common in females, 10 percent of cases detected are in males.

## WHAT CAUSES BULIMIA?

As with other eating disorders, there are many reasons why a person becomes bulimic. The illness often starts as a diet, however, when the person breaks the diet or does not lose weight, they feel miserable and binge on large amounts of food. They then try to get rid of it by vomiting or going to the bathroom. Bulimics frequently binge on cake, candy, or fatty foods—the very foods they want to cut out of their diet. The cycle of bingeing and purging can happen many times in one day. Bulimics often feel intense shame and **self-loathing** because of their eating disorder. Yet, despite these emotions, sufferers also feel powerless to stop their destructive cycle of behavior.

## IT HAPPENS

Statistically, bulimia is more common than anorexia, however, it is more difficult to identify because it is often a hidden illness. Sufferers feel ashamed of their problem and do not want anyone else to know about it, and the secrecy and shame can make them feel even more lonely and unhappy. They then turn to food for comfort, and then the cycle of bingeing and purging continues.

The cycle of bingeing and purging can happen many times in one day.

## BEING A COMPULSIVE EATER

Many people occasionally eat too many cookies, and they may also indulge in candy or have an extra portion of food. This does little harm. However, some people regularly binge. They are unable to control the urge to eat large quantities of food. They eat without feeling hunger or feeling full, and this excessive eating leads to weight gain. That in turn makes them feel unhappy. To blot out their unhappiness, they then eat more. **Compulsive** eaters eat for comfort and to escape painful emotions that are difficult to face. They constantly pick at food and feel unable to stop. Compulsive eaters do not eat because of physical hunger. Instead, food becomes a coping mechanism to deal with other problems.

Compulsive eating may make a person feel better while they eat. However, they often feel guilt and shame afterward.

Those who suffer from eating disorders are affected physically, but mentally, too. Research from NEDA shows that suicide rates are particularly high among people suffering from eating disorders.

# IT HAPPENS

Being on a diet that severely restricts food can mean that when a person breaks their diet, they overindulge in food. According to NEDA, teenage girls who diet frequently are 12 times more likely to binge than teenage girls who do not diet.

*Bulimics may spend a long time suffering in silence and feeling alone with their problems.*

## EATING IN SECRET

People who suffer from binge eating or compulsive eating disorders often eat alone because they are embarrassed about their behavior. They withdraw from regular socializing because they feel guilty and ashamed about their eating. This isolation makes them turn to food for comfort even more. Sufferers of these eating disorders often feel empty and inadequate, and eating makes them feel safe and comforted. However, when they are unable to stop bingeing or eating, they feel greater unhappiness with themselves. This leads to more bingeing and overeating. People who binge or eat compulsively become overweight. Being very overweight, or **obese**, can lead to health complications. These include heart problems, movement problems, and illnesses such as **diabetes**.

# I'm Too Scared to Eat

**SATURDAY JUNE 5**

I ate 1 piece of bread, 1 piece of chicken, and drank a glass of juice today. I'm so cold, even though it is hot outside. Mom says to put my swimsuit on and come outside. She is in the pool with my brother, and he's yelling at me to get in, too. I'm not going. I hate my body, and I'm not letting Mom see me without my clothes on. She keeps telling me I'm skinny, but I know I'm fat. She is just trying to make me fatter.

**THURSDAY JULY 1**

I ate 1 apple and 2 tomatoes today. A good day. And I ran for 20 minutes. I've lost 5 pounds.

I have to check my weight every day. I'm terrified of gaining.

### TUESDAY AUGUST 10

I feel really weird today. My hair is falling out in clumps, and my breath smells gross. Mom and Dad say they think I have an eating disorder. They took me to see a doctor, and she said I have anorexia nervosa. She weighed me. I'm 96 pounds (43 kg). The doctor says that is too low for my height—5 feet, 6 inches (1.5 m). I think it's too much. I'm too scared to eat now—I know it will just make me fatter.

### SUNDAY AUGUST 22

I'm frightened. I couldn't breathe today, and my heart felt funny. Then, I couldn't see and I fainted. Next thing I knew, I woke up in the hospital. The doctors say I'm really weak and **dehydrated**. I am on a **drip**. The doctors say that I need to gain weight and that I need special help to get better. I can't stop crying—I don't want to get fat. It's all I can think about, even though I know I am sick.

### MONDAY AUGUST 30

I've been moved to a clinic that specializes in eating disorders. The doctors say I have gained a few pounds and that they are happy with my progress. It feels really weird to hear them say gaining weight is a good thing. I still feel scared about it—and it feels bad.

### WEDNESDAY SEPTEMBER 15

I've made a friend—Kaitlin. She is in the room next to me. She has been anorexic for two years now. We talk about it, and how we feel. It is good to find someone who gets how I feel. We do a **group therapy** session, too, me, Kaitlin, and some other girls in here. It helps to talk. The doctors say if I can do that, I can learn not to use food to cover up my emotions. It's hard, and I still want to lose weight soooo bad.

The doctors told Mom it will take time for me to get better. Mom says I don't have to do it on my own—she has my back. She says to just focus on getting strong, then she is taking me on vacation. I said OK, but no beaches and bathing suits. I'm not ready for that yet ...

# CHAPTER TWO

# LIVING WITH AN EATING DISORDER

People struggling with anorexia nervosa usually suffer from several additional health complications. For example, they lose a lot of body fat. As a result, their body desperately tries to keep warm by growing a covering of downy hair. As the eating disorder's grip tightens, the hair of an anorexic may begin to thin and fall out. Their skin may also look dry and flaky.

## GETTING SICK

It is common for anorexics to feel faint and weak. This is because they do not eat enough food to sustain, or keep up, their energy levels. They feel cold, even on a warm day. As a result of not consuming nutrient-rich foods, the heart muscle becomes starved. It then begins to shrink and slow down. This can be extremely dangerous. As the heart slows down and the person's **blood pressure** drops, heart failure is a strong possibility.

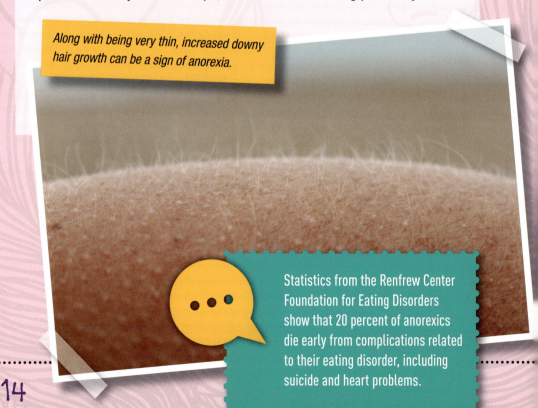

Along with being very thin, increased downy hair growth can be a sign of anorexia.

Statistics from the Renfrew Center Foundation for Eating Disorders show that 20 percent of anorexics die early from complications related to their eating disorder, including suicide and heart problems.

## PROBLEMS BUILD UP

The long-term effects of anorexia on a woman's body are incredibly serious. This is because being very underweight affects the **hormones** that are responsible for a woman's menstrual cycle. This means that anorexic teenagers may not start their periods at all, or their periods may stop for a long time. This can lead to **fertility** difficulties, and they may struggle to conceive, or become pregnant, when they are adults.

Both male and female anorexics also suffer from a bone disease called osteoporosis. This is because they do not have enough calcium in their bodies to keep their bones healthy and strong. Calcium is found in dairy products, such as cheese and milk. Without this **mineral**, bones become brittle and fragile. Even a simple fall can result in a broken or shattered bone.

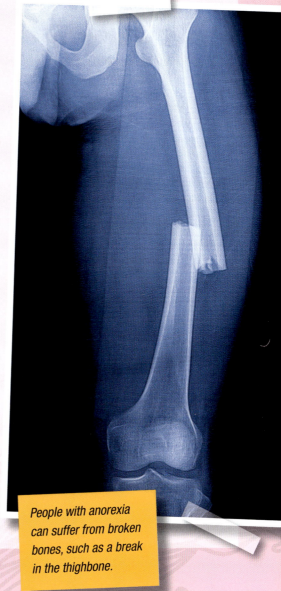

People with anorexia can suffer from broken bones, such as a break in the thighbone.

"I feel tired all the time, but I'm still too scared to eat."

## DAMAGING THE BODY

When someone vomits, acid produced in the stomach wears away at the protective layer of enamel that covers the teeth. As a result, bulimics often have discolored and rotting teeth. Stomach acid also causes a sore, burning throat. More seriously, it can damage an organ at the back of the throat called the esophagus. Through repeated vomiting, the esophagus can become very sore and infected. If the esophagus tears and blood appears in someone's vomit, it can be life-threatening.

Sufferers of eating disorders often take an excess of laxatives. Overuse of laxatives can lead to constant **constipation**. It can cause diarrhea and stomach pains. There is also a risk of a person becoming **addicted** to laxatives. If this happens, a person is unable defecate, or pass waste, normally, and may have embarrassing accidents.

## VISIBLE AND HIDDEN PROBLEMS

Regular vomiting upsets the body's natural chemical balances and causes dehydration. This results in dizziness and can lead to an irregular heartbeat and even heart failure. People with bulimia often feel tired as a result of dehydration, and their faces look puffy. Blood vessels in the eyes sometimes burst from the pressure of repeated vomiting. They may also have sores and blisters on their hands. These are caused by acid in their vomit irritating and burning the skin on their hands. Bulimics may have pressure marks from their teeth on their hands, created when they make themselves vomit.

People with bulimia, like those with anorexia, often lack essential nutrients. In the teenage years, the young body is developing quickly. A lack of vital nutrients can stunt the body's growth and development. In particular, laxatives and vomiting get rid of a very important mineral called potassium, which is essential for a healthy heart.

People with bulimia ... often lack essential nutrients.

# IT HAPPENED TO THEM

Little Mix's Jade Thirwall suffered from anorexia for five years before seeking help. Jade says that being anorexic made her feel in control, and that she would wear baggy clothes to hide her thin body. The star hid her illness from everyone around her but, eventually, Jade opened up and told someone about her problem. She was hospitalized to help her recover from her illness. Jade left the hospital just before she turned 18. She then auditioned for the hit TV show *The X Factor*. Jade went on to become a global superstar, proving that people can recover from eating disorders and lead successful lives.

*Even celebrities who appear very confident may be hiding their unhappiness and low **self-esteem**. Bulimia can affect anyone, whatever their lifestyle.*

A recent study showed that by the age of six, girls especially start to express concerns about their own weight or shape. From 40 to 60 percent of elementary schoolgirls are concerned about their weight or about becoming too fat. This concern may endure through life.

17

## PUNISHING THEMSELVES

People who suffer from eating disorders often feel ashamed and hate themselves for what they are doing. They know that their eating pattern is not making them happy. However, they feel unable stop. Their eating disorder becomes a punishment for their behavior.

Even though sufferers' eating may be out of control with bingeing and purging, people with eating disorders often feel that this is one area of their lives over which they have control. Their eating disorder makes them feel safe. Food is used as a coping mechanism to deal with feelings and concerns that the sufferers may not be able to express to other people or even face up to. Sufferers are also often trying to cope with depression or other anxiety disorders.

*People with eating disorders are tormented by their desperation to break free from the cycle of their eating pattern.*

According to the National Institute of Mental Health (NIMH), boys and men are increasingly suffering from eating disorders. However, the shame they often feel from being associated with what was considered a "girls' disease" makes them reluctant to ask for professional help.

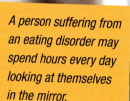

A person suffering from an eating disorder may spend hours every day looking at themselves in the mirror.

## IT HAPPENS

A *People* magazine telephone poll reported that 80 percent of females surveyed said that women in movies and television programs made them feel insecure about their bodies.

### FAMOUS AND SUFFERING

Several high-profile celebrities such as Taylor Swift and Lily Collins have admitted to struggling with eating disorders, including bulimia. They hope that it will help other people feel brave enough to own up to their problem and seek the necessary help. However, it is important not to think that bulimia cannot be all that bad because celebrities seem to have such glamorous lives. It is crucial to remember how desperate any eating disorder makes a person feel, even if they look good and lead a high-profile celebrity life.

## UNDER PRESSURE

Eating disorders put enormous pressure on friends and family. They often feel helpless and desperate when they see a loved one struggling with a troubled relationship with food. Those suffering from eating disorders often try to hide their illness. They may pretend to be **allergic** to certain foods. They may make an excuse about having eaten earlier, so they do not have to eat in public. People with anorexia go to extreme lengths to hide their food. They may secrete it under the table, in bags, or inside their clothes. Those with bulimia and binge eaters may hide and stash food. They then eat it secretly when no one is watching. Family and friends may not notice the hidden food. However, they do notice a loved one's changing mental health. They see them becoming withdrawn, unhappy, and isolated from their friends and family.

Sufferers of eating disorders often avoid social situations. They may be terrified of eating in public or can't bear to miss out on an exercise session.

Female high school athletes who suffer from an eating disorder are twice as likely to develop a **musculoskeletal** injury as athletes who are not suffering from any form of eating disorder.

## TORMENTED BY FOOD

**Social interaction** is an incredibly important part of life. Most young people enjoy chatting with friends, arranging to meet for a milkshake, or hanging out in the park. Many of these social arrangements may involve food, such as eating out or going over to a friend's house for a meal. For most teenagers, these types of activity are a fun part of everyday life. However, they pose huge problems for sufferers of eating disorders. For them, these regular activities are filled with terror. Their minds will be full of questions and thoughts, such as how will they avoid food; will they eat too much; and will anyone notice them pretending to eat? Those who suffer from eating disorders are continually tormented by thoughts of eating or not eating.

## IT HAPPENS

Exercising and keeping fit is an important part of maintaining a healthy body and mind. However, people suffering from eating disorders often go to extremes exercising in order to burn off any calories they have eaten. For example, a tiny portion of food may make them feel that they have to do hundreds of jumping jacks to get rid of the calories they have eaten. This kind of intense exercise can be damaging to their health. For example, it can put a weakened heart under even more pressure. Brittle bones can break more easily with intense exercise.

"I stopped going to friends' houses—I was too worried that they'd try and make me eat."

# It's All I've Got!

### SATURDAY SEPTEMBER 11

Since Dad left, nothing has been the same. I'm so down; why did he do that to us? I hate him. Mom keeps asking me to come out of my room, but I just want to stay in here. Away from her and Max and Kai, my annoying little brothers. The only thing that makes me feel better is eating and eating, then throwing it all up. Mom knows something is wrong. She keeps crying and asking me to talk to her. But I can't. I just say "I'm fine, stop nagging!" and "Please just leave me alone."

### FRIDAY OCTOBER 8

Today, Mom made me go to the doctor. He asked me if I was feeling OK. And I told him a load of lies: that I was fine and nothing was upsetting me. He typed up some notes, and said OK, well, come back if you need anything else. Mom was mad. But, I can't tell her the truth about what's going on. If she knows, she'll try and stop me. And it's all I've got!

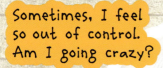

Sometimes, I feel so out of control. Am I going crazy?

Mom made me go on another beach vacation this year. Max and Kai had a great time, of course, but I hated it. I don't want anyone to see my body.

### SATURDAY DECEMBER 4

I'm scared. I threw up blood this morning, and I had really bad stomach cramps. Mom heard me crying in the bathroom and banged on the door. I couldn't take it anymore. I told her the truth—that I've been bingeing then making myself vomit. Mom hugged me and cried with me. She told me she loves me, and she is gonna help me get better. She thinks it's her fault, because her and Dad got divorced. I'm glad I told Mom now—I don't feel so alone anymore.

When I feel bad, I eat and eat. Then I feel really scared that I've eaten so much. I feel gross, like, what's wrong with me? I'm so disgusting. I'll get fat, I know it. So, I put my fingers down my throat and I throw it all up. Then I feel better, calmer. Sometimes I cry afterward. It's like everything I'm feeling comes out in a rush. And then I feel exhausted. Just numb.

# CHAPTER THREE

# WHY DO TEENS GET EATING DISORDERS?

Adolescents are particularly vulnerable to developing eating disorders. This is because teenagers have a lot to deal with. Their bodies and minds are going through many physical changes as they mature. These changes can be difficult. For example, if they have a rush of hormones, it can put them on a roller-coaster ride of emotions.

## GROWING UP IS TOUGH

There are also many social issues that can affect young people, including problems at home, difficulties at school, or issues with friends. Some teenagers cannot cope with these problems. Instead of dealing with them, they try to blot out their pain with disordered, or abnormal, eating patterns. Many teenagers are often unaware that they are using food as a way of coping. However, the painful truth is that an eating disorder does not get rid of other problems, such as a family breakups or bullying. It just adds to the unhappiness.

*Going through **puberty** and the changes that it brings to the body can be a frightening experience for teens.*

When researchers followed a group of 496 adolescent girls from the age of 8 until they were 20 years old, they found that 18.4 percent of the girls had suffered from some kind of eating disorder during their teenage years.

*Teenage troubles, such as bullying at school, can have serious consquences.*

Some teenagers do not want to face the responsibilities and challenges of the adult world—they do not feel ready for them. For example, girls going through puberty often do not want their bodies to develop grown-up curves and a more rounded shape. By being underweight, they can chain their bodies to childhood.

## IT HAPPENS

A research study by the NIMH indicated that physical changes, along with **psychological** changes, during puberty may be related to the development of bulimia and binge eating in young teenagers.

Teenagers have a lot to deal with.

## BULLYING AND EATING DISORDERS

Bullying comes in many forms. These include name-calling. They also include unkind comments on social networking sites and excluding someone from friendship groups. Bullying can be extremely destructive. It lowers self-esteem and makes a person feel isolated and frightened. Cruel teasing about weight is a form of bullying. The danger of this type of bullying is that it can trigger a person to embark on a very restrictive diet. This can quickly escalate into anorexia nervosa.

"Being thin made me feel good."

Young people are heavily influenced by social media and information that they find online. Sites that promote eating disorders and encourage unhealthy eating habits can make a person's problems far worse.

## TEASING IS NOT HARMLESS

When bullies tease people about their looks, they may make the comments as a joke. They may even think that the comments are harmless. However, they can be devastating for the victim, who turns the negative feelings toward their relationship with food. Of course, many people who experience bullying do not develop eating disorders. However, for others, it is the trigger that causes an agonizing and lonely relationship with food. Any kind of bullying lowers victims' self-esteem, and low self-esteem lies at the root of many eating disorders. Whether it is mental or physical aggression, bullying has long-lasting effects. Often, by the time the bully has stopped, the sufferer may be caught up in an eating disorder that spirals out of control.

## IT HAPPENS

Some forms of social networking and some websites try to encourage people into a life of eating problems. They promote eating disorders, such as anorexia, calling them lifestyle choices. These sites taunt people to lose more and more weight. They ignore the physical and emotional harm caused by eating disorders.

Research has shown that if overweight young people are victimized, they are less likely to participate in physical activity. They will often have negative attitudes about sports. Studies also show that among overweight and obese adults, those who were or are bullied over their weight are more likely to be diagnosed with a binge eating disorder.

## PRESSURE TO LOOK GOOD

Adolescents face not only a lot of **peer** pressure, but also media pressure to behave and look a certain way. Many begin to believe that having a slim body is all that matters to anyone. People with eating disorders often project all their hopes onto their body shape. They believe that if they are thinner, they will be happier. Although they may be a healthy weight, when they look in the mirror, they see someone who is fat. This dissatisfaction with body image continues the unhealthy cycle of dieting and bingeing.

## PARTICULARLY AT RISK

Athletes and teenagers who participate in activities such as dance and sports, in which body image is important, are particularly vulnerable to eating disorders. In the early 2000s, a study of runners found that of 184 female athletes, 16 percent had an eating disorder. Today, those working with teenagers, such as coaches and teachers, are trained to spot signs of possible problems and offer support where needed.

## IT HAPPENED TO THEM

Many gymnasts have spoken out about how the pressure to be thin led to them developing eating disorders. Shawn Johnson and Cathy Rigby are just two of the world-class athletes who have revealed that they suffered from disordered eating patterns, including anorexia and bulimia, in an attempt to maintain a "perfect" body shape during their careers.

Adolescents face a lot of peer pressure ... to look a certain way.

Dancers are often under a lot of pressure to maintain a particular shape and weight.

Although most athletes diagnosed with eating disorders are female, studies have shown that male athletes are also at risk. Those competing in sports that tend to emphasize diet, appearance, size, and weight are especially vulnerable. These sports include weight-class sports such as wrestling, rowing, and horse racing. They also include **aesthetic** sports such as bodybuilding.

# I Can't Stop Eating

**WEDNESDAY JANUARY 6**

It's midnight, and I just can't sleep. I keep thinking about Kayla and Amy, and how they are so mean to me at school. I just want to eat to keep me from feeling so sad ...

I've just eaten a whole package of cookies. I feel so gross. I ate one, then another, and then another. I just stuffed them into my mouth, and I hardly chewed before I swallowed them. It felt so good while I was eating, like I was just lost in the food and it blotted out all the mean words. Then, after, when

I saw the empty package, I couldn't believe what I had done. What is wrong with me? Why can't I stop myself? I am gross, stupid, and ugly—just like Kayla says.

Kayla and Amy say I don't have any friends because I gross everyone out. I wish I was cute and popular, like them.

## MONDAY FEBRUARY 1

Today was just the worst. It was my sister's (Zoe's) birthday. Mom invited my aunts, uncles, and cousins over—yup, the whole family. My aunt kept looking at me, and I know she thinks I look fat. I've gained so much weight. Mom doesn't say anything. Neither does Dad. He never notices me anyway —all he thinks about is work. I hate him. I hate myself, too. Why would anyone love me anyway? I'm too gross.

I hardly ate while everyone was here. Then, later, I ate handfuls of Zoe's cake in secret. Mom didn't say anything when she put the cake away. I know she knows something is wrong with me. Maybe she just doesn't care.

## MONDAY MARCH 8

Kayla and Amy were so mean to me again today at school. They told everyone I'm the fattest person in class and that I have to wear supersized clothes because I eat supersized food. I cried all the way home. I went into the bathroom, and all I could see in the mirror was a big, fat, ugly monster. I opened the cabinet, and I saw Mom's pills. I've just swallowed a handful of them. I just want to go to sleep so I don't have to be here.

## TUESDAY MARCH 9

I'm in the hospital. Mom won't stop crying. Her face is all blotchy. Zoe is crying, too. Even Dad has red eyes. The doctors told Mom and Dad that they think I need some help, some counseling. Mom gave me a big hug then. She says she loves me, Dad loves me, too. Even Zoe loves me! I told Mom that I can't stop eating, and I hate myself. Mom hugged me harder and told me that she will always love me, and that if I can learn to love myself even half as much as she does, everything will be OK ...

# CHAPTER FOUR

# HOW PEOPLE GET BETTER

People who suffer from eating disorders are often extremely secretive about their condition. They may go to great lengths to cover up their problem. As a result, the eating disorder may continue unchecked by a medical professional for a very long time. It is often not until family and friends finally recognize that there is something wrong that a diagnosis takes place.

## ADMITTING TO THE PROBLEM

Sufferers are often reluctant to admit that they have a problem with food. However, research shows that the early treatment of eating disorders increases the speed and likelihood of recovery. The longer a person is caught in the grips of an eating disorder, the harder it can be for them to break free. That is why it is so crucial for people to recognize the main signs of an eating disorder in family or friends, or even themselves.

*Therapists* trained to understand eating disorders can help people suffering from them.

## IN THE FAMILY?

Scientists are researching possible **biological** causes of eating disorders. For example, in some individuals with eating disorders, certain chemicals in the brain that control hunger, appetite, and digestion have been found to be unbalanced. Eating disorders often run in families, and current research suggests that there may be a **genetic** link.

## HOW TO SPOT AN EATING DISORDER

The signs that a person may have, or may be developing, an eating disorder include:

- low self-esteem, constantly putting themselves down
- constantly referring to weight or body shape
- avoiding meals and making excuses about not eating
- becoming very particular about order and tidiness, getting upset if things are not in the correct place
- spending a lot of time in the bathroom
- wearing baggy clothes in an attempt to disguise weight loss.

If a person displays some of these signs, it may be an indication that they have an eating disorder. By understanding and recognizing the signs, family members and friends of a sufferer may be able to step in and encourage the person to get help.

A survey found that up to 40 percent of overweight girls and 37 percent of overweight boys are teased about their weight by peers or family members. This teasing often leads to weight gain, binge eating, and extreme weight control measures.

## NO QUICK FIX

There is no quick fix for an eating disorder. Some people think sufferers just need to eat regular, reasonable meals to "cure" themselves. However, that is incredibly difficult and often impossible for someone with an eating disorder to do. A person with an eating disorder has a **distorted** way of thinking about food. It takes specialized support to unlock it, so that the sufferer can learn how to eat for health again. Recovery from an eating disorder takes time. It involves addressing both an individual's physical and emotional needs. The person has to find new ways of dealing with the stresses and challenges of their life, without using food as a coping mechanism.

*Meditation* and relaxing exercise, such as yoga, can help people manage their stress.

Being overly concerned with weight poses a significant threat to a person's psychological and physical health. It has been documented as a significant risk factor for depression, low self-esteem, and body dissatisfaction.

## FEELING GOOD

Positive self-esteem helps prevent eating disorders and supports a person's recovery. Recovery from eating disorders is about learning to accept oneself and to nourish the body. Avoiding diets helps a person concentrate on healthy eating rather than trying to become thin or to eliminate complete food groups. **Nutritionists** can give sufferers specific advice and support about how to create a healthy and well-balanced diet.

The road to recovery from an eating disorder is a long one. It has many emotional and physical ups and downs. It is important to support individuals and help them realize that while there may be setbacks and disappointments in their recovery, it does not mean that they have failed.

*Feeling good about yourself and how you look is called positive body image. Friends can encourage each other to love the way they look.*

## IT HAPPENS

Statistics from the Alliance for Eating Disorders Awareness show that 90 percent of those who have eating disorders are females between the ages of 12 and 25. An estimated 11 percent of high school students have been diagnosed with an eating disorder. Anorexia is the third-most common chronic illness among adolescents. A chronic illness is one that is persistent and long-lasting.

## DIFFERENT BODIES

Everyone is different and unique, with special qualities to offer and share. There is no perfect person or perfect body shape. Everyone has flaws, and it is important for people to learn to accept their flaws without judging themselves too harshly. It is also useful to challenge media presentations of girls and women, as well as boys and men. NEDA research suggests that the public see more than 3,000 commercials each day containing messages that encourage girls and women to feel unhappy with their bodies.

Today, people are better informed about the dangers of eating disorders. It is important that young people also feel confident about their bodies, whatever their size and shape.

Many young girls start their dieting spiral because commercials advertising weight-loss products promise a body that is perfect by media standards. However, one analysis of weight-loss advertising found that more than half of all advertising for weight-loss products made use of claims that are not backed up with evidence.

## GETTING BETTER

The first step to recovery is admitting that there is a problem. Some people receive inpatient treatment either in the hospital or in a center that specializes in eating disorders. There, their food intake is closely monitored to make sure that their bodies are recovering. Counseling encourages sufferers to talk about their emotions and find ways to deal with their problems. This may include family therapy, which often helps sufferers and their families deal with problems that may have contributed to the eating disorder. One of the most difficult decisions to make when a person is life-threateningly underweight is whether or not to force-feed them. Parents of young people are usually allowed to make that difficult decision. However, the issue is more complex when doctors are treating adults, because anorexics often do not even want a drip put into their body to rehydrate, or put fluids back into, them because they fear that the fluid will make them gain weight.

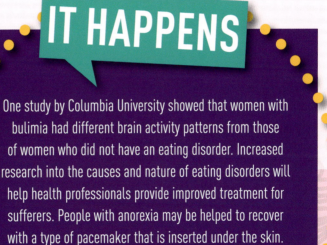

# IT HAPPENS

One study by Columbia University showed that women with bulimia had different brain activity patterns from those of women who did not have an eating disorder. Increased research into the causes and nature of eating disorders will help health professionals provide improved treatment for sufferers. People with anorexia may be helped to recover with a type of pacemaker that is inserted under the skin. This sends electrical impulses to an area of the brain linked to appetite and mood. A study in Canada showed an improvement in the condition of the patients who were treated with the pacemaker.

# I Feel in Control

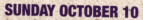

### SATURDAY JUNE 5

Mom is on a diet again. She says she needs to lose a few pounds, and it's important to eat low-cal foods. She has to cut back on her eating. Mom says we can diet together, and it will be fun—we'll both be a size zero by Christmas! Then, she told me I could do with losing a few pounds … Thanks, Mom! Why does she always have to make me feel so bad? I couldn't stop looking in the mirror after that—perhaps I do look too big?

### MONDAY AUGUST 9

I'm so much better than Mom at losing weight! I've lost 8 pounds already! Mom is jealous. I like how that makes me feel. I feel in control, like I'm the best at something —better than her! It feels like I'm getting my own back for Mom being mean to me.

### SUNDAY OCTOBER 10

I'm really tired today. It was hard at school, and everyone got mad at me during the swim meet. I let the team down because I was too tired to swim. They told me I'm getting skinny, and I need to eat so I can compete. But I don't want to get fat again. Being skinny is so much better, even if I am a little tired.

### FRIDAY NOVEMBER 5

Mom says she is really worried. She says I'm too thin, and I never eat enough. She tried to make me eat at breakfast, but I just hid the food in my pocket when she wasn't looking, then threw it in the garbage later. I've lost another 8 pounds. I am so frightened to eat now. I know it will make me fat.

Mom is always nagging at me to do better at everything—but I'll show her I can lose weight the best!

## SATURDAY DECEMBER 11

Today, I passed out at school, and my teacher called Mom. She took me to the doctor. He said I have anorexia and am dangerously sick. He signed me into the clinic for treatment. Mom kept crying and saying it is all her fault for starting that stupid diet. I know Mom didn't mean for the diet to end up this way, but I'm wondering about how she has made me feel ...

## MONDAY JANUARY 3

In therapy today, I talked about food and why I like the feeling of being thin and not eating. It makes me feel like I am in control and nothing can hurt me. The therapist says I'm using dieting to help me deal with difficult feelings. He says that I need to learn to use other ways to express how I feel.

He wants Mom to come in over the next few weeks and talk about our relationship, so I can tell her how bad she makes me feel sometimes. I'm scared about hurting Mom, but I know if I want to get better, I need to learn to say how I feel and not use food to show it.

# CHAPTER FIVE

# KEEPING WELL

**Beyond Stereotypes was a study commissioned by Dove, a major manufacturer of beauty and hygiene products. It surveyed 3,300 girls and women between the ages of 15 and 64 in 10 countries. The study discovered that 67 percent of all women in this age group stopped certain activities because they felt unhappy about their looks.**

## NO MORE SIZE ZERO

Condé Nast is an international publisher of *Vogue* and other magazines. The publisher has declared that its editors will not use models who are so thin that they look like they have eating disorders. This is because many people believe that the use of such thin models adds to young people's feelings of dissatisfaction with their own bodies and can start the cycle of dieting that so often leads to disordered eating patterns.

The use of ultrathin models puts pressure on girls and boys to look a certain way.

"When I looked in magazines, I wanted to be as thin as the models I saw."

## THE IDEAL BODY

Western society presents an image of a so-called ideal body that is far from the reality of most people. For example, clothes are designed for thin women and modeled by women with a specific body shape. According to the Renfrew Center Foundation for Eating Disorders, the body type portrayed in advertising as the ideal is possessed naturally by only 5 percent of American females. Eating disorders often stem from low self-esteem. Therefore, taking control over food (or losing control over it) is used to dull the unhappiness that the person feels. However, an eating disorder only buries the cause of the unhappiness—it doesn't solve it. The media has an important role in helping boys and girls focus on their qualities and strengths as people, rather than their weight and body image.

*Many people argue that magazine publishers have a responsibility to use models of an average size and shape.*

Social media has a huge influence on how teenagers view themselves and others. According to Common Sense Media, 41 percent of teenage girls say they use social media to "make themselves look cooler." Another study of teenage girls found that social media users were significantly more likely than non-social media users to have a drive for thinness and to watch their weight.

## LEARNING TO BE WELL

People suffering from eating disorders find it extremely difficult to judge clearly what is a reasonable amount of food for a healthy body. That is because they no longer recognize what normal eating is. It takes time and patience for sufferers to recover a sense of **perspective**. They need support to accept and understand that the body needs a balance of carbohydrates, fats, and protein. It also needs **vitamins** and minerals, as well as a reasonable amount of exercise to keep fit and healthy. People with eating disorders need to relearn how to eat for health and well-being.

## MODERN PROBLEMS

Eating disorders are on the rise, but so is childhood obesity. This stems from unhealthy diets and not enough exercise. Programs to reduce obesity are extremely important because obesity puts young people at a greater risk of developing many serious illnesses, such as diabetes and heart disease. However, it is also important not

Being underweight can have serious health consequences. However, obesity is a problem now for many young people too.

People with eating disorders need to relearn how to eat for health and well-being.

to create anxiety and worry among children about their body shape and image. That can then lead to a cycle of harmful eating disorders. Society has a responsibility to make sure that young people understand that healthy eating is about balanced, nutritious meals and not about a spiral of diets.

Learning how to have a balanced attitude to food and eating is important. A little fast food, such as pizza or a hamburger, every now and again is absolutely fine.

A study found that social media use is linked to self-objectification. This is when people see themselves as objects for use, rather than as human beings. Using social media for just 30 minutes a day can change the way a person views their own body.

# Getting Better

### SHELLY'S STORY
### WEDNESDAY MARCH 9

It's been a year now since I left the clinic. It took time for me to get better, and it was really hard. I had good days and bad days. Some days I panicked about putting on weight. Then, I had days when I laughed with Kaitlin and forgot all about food. And then the best day came—I left the clinic and went home.

Mom has been great, she and I are so much closer. And we are going on vacation in a couple of months with Kaitlin. I know I have a long way to go, but I'm starting to see food as something that my body needs. And I'm learning not to be scared to eat.

### MASON'S STORY
### TUESDAY AUGUST 10

When Dad found out how sick I'd been, he moved to a house nearby so I could see him more. Spending time with him felt good. We went to family therapy, too, with Mom, and I had counseling. Talking helped—when I feel angry now, I tell Dad or Mom or my counselor. I still feel like bingeing sometimes, but I try and use other things to get past it. I've started going to a boxing club—my coach says hitting a punch bag is healthier than hurting my body. I still have days when I feel bad, but bulimia's not all I've got anymore.

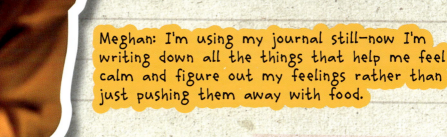

Meghan: I'm using my journal still—now I'm writing down all the things that help me feel calm and figure out my feelings rather than just pushing them away with food.

## MEGHAN'S STORY
### TUESDAY JULY 6

Seeing Mom and Dad so upset at the hospital made me realize that they do care about me. I thought no one loved me and that I wasn't good enough, so I'm trying to work on that now. My counselor tells me that when I look in the mirror, I need to tell myself all the things that are good about me, rather than calling myself names and telling myself I am fat. It sounds corny, but it does help. I'm trying to eat more normally, too, and I'm trying to stop eating in secret.

When I feel like eating and eating, I take deep breaths or tell Mom how I feel. When she gives me a hug, it makes everything so much better. My cousin Shelby has been great, too. She keeps saying that I'm really pretty. It feels nice. I just have to start believing it now!

## RACHEL'S STORY
### SUNDAY MAY 8

Mom and I are getting along a lot better now. The therapy has helped her understand that the things she was saying to me were affecting how I feel about myself. Mom says it has also helped her understand more about how she feels about herself and her own body, and that we can work on making each other feel good rather than dieting to be a size zero.

I still find it hard not to think about my weight. When I panic about it, I try and think about all the things I want to do in the future. I'm working on going to dance college, and I want to be well enough to do that next year. When I dance, I try and think about my body being strong, rather than trying to keep it from getting bigger. I'm learning to be in control without using food.

# GLOSSARY

**addicted** dependant on particular substances, such as food, drugs, or alcohol

**aesthetic** related to appearance

**allergic** an extreme reaction to a food or other substance

**binge** to rapidly consume a large amount of food

**biological** related to processes within the body

**blood pressure** the pressure of blood in the circulatory system

**calorie** the measurement of energy in food

**compulsive** unable to stop doing something

**constipation** having difficulty passing feces, or waste

**dehydrated** having lost an abnormal amount of water from the body

**depression** a mental illness that causes severe sadness

**diabetes** a condition in which the body cannot control the amount of sugar in its bloodstream

**diagnosed** identified an illness

**distorted** not accurate, out of shape

**drip** a device that provides the body with substances it needs via a tube inserted into a vein

**fertility** related to a person's ability to conceive children

**genetic** related to genes, the basic units of heredity

**group therapy** a form of counseling in which more than one person participates

**hormones** substances that control actions in the body

**laxatives** pills that encourage a person's bowels to pass feces, or waste

**mechanism** a system

**meditation** a method used to calm the body and mind

**mineral** an element in food that the body needs for healthy growth and development

**musculoskeletal** related to both the muscles and skeleton

**nourishment** the substances and energy provided by food and which keep the body healthy

**nutrients** elements in food that provide the body with energy

**nutritionists** people who study food and how it affects the body

**obese** dangerously overweight

**obsessed** constantly thinking about something

**peer** a person of a similar age

**perspective** a point of view

**psychological** related to the mind

**puberty** the physical and emotional changes that occur as children develop into adults

**self-esteem** pride in or respect for oneself

**self-loathing** hating oneself

**social interaction** talking to and spending time with other people

**therapists** people who are trained to help others talk about their emotional problems

**vitamins** substances found in foods that are essential for the normal and healthy working of the body

# FIND OUT MORE

## BOOKS

Cusido, Carmen. *Coping with Eating Disorders* (Coping). Rosen Publishing, 2019.

Landau, Jennifer. *Teens Talk About Body Image and Eating Disorders* (Teen Voices: Real Teens Discuss Real Problems). Rosen Publishing, 2018.

Petro-Roy, Jen. *You Are Enough: Your Guide to Body Image and Eating Disorder Recovery*. Feiwel & Friends, 2019.

## WEBSITES

Find out more about eating disorders at:
**kidshealth.org/en/teens/eat-disorder.html**

Discover how you can help someone with an eating disorder at:
**www.helpguide.org/articles/eating-disorders/helping-someone-with-an-eating-disorder.htm**

Learn about eating disorders and what causes them at:
**www.psychiatry.org/patients-families/eating-disorders**

## ORGANIZATIONS

Teen Line
Cedars-Sinai
P.O. Box 48750
Los Angeles, CA 90048
(310) 855-HOPE (4673) or
(800) TLC-TEEN (852-8336)
**Website: teenlineonline.org**
If you are struggling with an eating disorder, or know someone who is, help is out there. Connect and get support at this great help site for teenagers.

### PUBLISHER'S NOTE TO EDUCATORS AND PARENTS:

All the websites featured above have been carefully reviewed to ensure that they are suitable for students. However, many websites change often, and we cannot guarantee that a site's future contents will continue to meet our high standards of educational value. Please be advised that students should be closely monitored whenever they access the Internet.

# INDEX

## ABOUT THE AUTHORS

Sarah Eason has authored many nonfiction books for children and has a special interest in young people's health and social issues. Sarah Levete has written hundreds of information books for children on a wide variety of subjects, including health and well-being.